PRIMARY SOURCES OF FAMOUS PEOPLE IN AMERICAN HISTORY™

ABIGAIL ADAMS

FAMOUS FIRST LADY
DESTACADA PRIMERA DAMA

MAYA GLASS

TRADUCCIÓN AL ESPAÑOL:
TOMÁS GONZÁLEZ

rosen central
Primary Source™
Editorial Buenas Letras™

The Rosen Publishing Group, Inc., New York

Published in 2004 by The Rosen Publishing Group, Inc.
29 East 21st Street, New York, NY 10010

First Bilingual Edition 2004
First English Edition 2004

Cataloging Data

Glass, Maya
Abigail Adams /Maya Glass; translation into Spanish Tomás González.— 1st ed.
    p. cm. — (Primary Sources of famous people in American history)
Summary: Introduces the life of Abigail Adams, the wife of President John Adams, who was much more independent than many women of her time, running a farm in her husband's absence and speaking and writing about women's rights.
Includes bibliographical references and index.
ISBN 0-8239-4148-5 (lib. bdg.)
1. Adams, Abigail, 1744-1818—Juvenile literature. 2. Presidents' spouses—United States—Biography—Juvenile literature. 3. Adams, John, 1735-1826—Juvenile literature. [1. Adams, Abigail, 1744-1818. 2. First ladies. 3. Women—Biography .4. Spanish Language Materials—Bilingual]
I. Title. II. Series: Primary sources of famous people in American history.
Bilingual.E322.1.A38 G55 2004
973.4'4'092—dc21

Manufactured in the United States of America

Photo credits: cover, pp. 5, 9, 13 Courtesy of The Massachusetts Historical Society; p. 7 Courtesy of Map Division, The New York Public Library, Astor, Lenox and Tilden Foundations; p.11 © A.G.K., Berlin/SuperStock Inc.; pp. 15, 21(bottom) Library of Congress, Geography and Map Division; p. 17 © Burstein Collection/Corbis; p. 19 Pennsylvania Academy of the Fine Arts, Philadelphia/The Bridgeman Art Library; p. 21(top) National Portrait Gallery, Smithsonian Institution/Art Resource, NY; p. 23 © Hulton/Archive/Getty Images; p. 25 Independence National Historical Park; p. 27 (top) Picture Collection, The Branch Libraries, The New York Public Library, Astor, Lenox and Tilden Foundations; p. 27 (bottom) © Bettman/Corbis; p. 29 U.S. Department of the Interior, National Parks Service, Adams National Historic Park.

Designer: Thomas Forget; Editor: Mark Beyer; Photo Researcher: Peter Tomlinson

CONTENTS

CONTENIDO

1 AN OUTSTANDING WOMAN

Abigail Adams was the wife of John Adams, America's second president. The wife of the president is called the first lady. Abigail Adams lived during an exciting period in history. She was also the mother of John Quincy Adams. He became the sixth president in 1825.

1 UNA MUJER EXCEPCIONAL

Abigail Adams fue la esposa de John Adams, el segundo presidente de Estados Unidos. A la mujer del presidente se le llama "primera dama". Abigail Adams vivió durante un período muy interesante de la historia. Además fue la madre de John Quincy Adams, quien en 1825 se convirtió en el sexto presidente del país.

Abigail Adams is shown here in a portrait from 1766. She was already a strong-minded woman.

Retrato de Abigail Adams en 1766. Ya entonces era una mujer resuelta.

When Abigail was young, America was not yet a country. During her life, the American Revolution was fought. In it, a group of colonies gained freedom from Great Britain. The United States of America was formed. John Adams traveled often to help form the country. Abigail wrote many letters to her husband when he was away.

Cuando Abigail era joven, Estados Unidos aún no era un país. Durante su vida se libró la Guerra de Independencia. En ella, un grupo de colonias se liberaron de Gran Bretaña y crearon los Estados Unidos de América. John Adams viajaba con frecuencia para ayudar a construir el país. Abigail le escribió muchas cartas cuando él estaba lejos de casa.

Shown on this 1783 map are the first thirteen colonies. Abigail and John Adams wanted the colonies to break from British rule.

En este mapa de 1783 aparecen los primeros trece colonias. Abigail y John Adams querían que las colonias se independizaran del gobierno británico.

Abigail's letters shared her ideas about slavery and women's rights. These letters are important American readings. Abigail Adams spoke against what she felt was wrong. Many women did not do that then. At the time, women's ideas were not considered equal to those of men. John Adams talked to Abigail about everything.

En sus cartas, Abigail expuso sus ideas sobre la esclavitud y los derechos de las mujeres. Estas cartas son importantes documentos históricos de Estados Unidos. Abigail Adams habló contra lo que creía equivocado. No muchas mujeres hacían eso en aquella época. En aquel entonces se consideraba que las ideas de las mujeres no eran iguales a las de los hombres. John Adams hablaba con Abigail de todos los temas.

the House and Furniture of the Solisiter General have fallen a pray to their own mericiless party— Surely the very firends of Administration, whilst they Detest the paricide & traitor—

I feel very differently at the approach of spring to what I did a month ago. We knew not then whether we could plant or sow with safety, whether when we had toild we could reap the fruits of our own industry, whether we could rest in our own Cottages, or whether we should not be driven from the Sea coasts to seek shelter in the wilderness, but now we feel as if we might sit under our own vine and eat the good of the Land— I feel a gaieti de Coar to which before I was a Stranger. I think the Sun looks brighter, the Birds sing more melodiously & Nature puts on a more chearfull countanance. We feel a temporary peace, & the fugitives are returning to their deserted habitations.

tho we felicitate ourselves, we sympathize with those who are trembling least the fate of Boston should be theirs— But they cannot be in Similar circumstances unless pusillanimity & cowardise should take possession of them— They have time & warning given them to see the Evil & shun it— I long to hear that you have declared an independancy— and by the way in the new code of Laws which I suppose it will be necessary for you to make I desire you would Remember the Ladies, & be more generous & favourable to them than your ancestors. Do not put such unlimited power into the hands of the Husbands. Remember all Men would be tyrants if they could. If perticuliar care & attention is not paid to the Ladies we are determined to foment a Rebelion, and will not hold ourselves bound by any Laws in which we have no voice, or Representation— That your Sex are Naturally Tyrannical is a Truth so thoroughly established as to admit of no Dispute, but such of you as wish to be happy willingly give up the harsh title of Master for the more tender & endearing one of Friend

---

In this letter, Abigail asks her husband to think about the rights of women.

Carta de Abigail a John Adams en la que le pide que tenga en cuenta los derechos de las mujeres.

9

2 EARLY YEARS

Abigail Smith was born on November 11, 1744. Abigail wanted to go to school, but she never got the chance. She read books and newspapers and kept a diary. Later she met John Adams, who shared her love of learning. John and Abigail first met in 1759. They started writing to each other. They fell in love through sharing their ideas in letters.

2 PRIMEROS AÑOS

Abigail Smith nació el 11 de noviembre de 1744. Abigail quería ir a la escuela pero nunca pudo hacerlo. Leía libros y revistas y escribía un diario. Después conoció a John Adams, con quien compartía el amor por el conocimiento. John y Abigail se conocieron en 1759. Empezaron a escribirse, compartieron sus ideas en las cartas y se enamoraron.

Abigail did not get a formal education as a young girl. She read a lot of books. She found many other ways to educate herself.

Cuando era niña, Abigail no recibió una educación formal. Pero Abigail leyó numerosos libros y encontró muchas maneras de educarse.

John and Abigail married in 1764. John Adams was a lawyer. He also had a farm in Massachusetts. He enjoyed working on his farm and being with Abigail. Their first child, named Nabby, was born in 1765. Abigail bore four more children by 1772. Abigail enjoyed raising and educating her children.

John y Abigail se casaron en 1764. John Adams era abogado y además tenía una granja en Massachusetts. Le gustaba estar con Abigail y trabajar en la granja. En 1765 tuvieron una niña a la que llamaron Nabby. En 1772 Abigail tenía ya cuatro hijos más. Abigail disfrutaba criando y educando a sus hijos.

This drawing shows the Adamses' farm in Braintree, Massachusetts.

Dibujo de la granja de la familia Adams en Braintree, Massachusetts.

Soon the family moved to Boston. John wanted to spend more time on politics. Britain was taxing its colonies heavily. One of the items taxed was tea. Abigail thought the tax was unfair. She decided to serve coffee in her house instead of tea.

Muy pronto la familia se mudó a Boston. John quería dedicarle más tiempo a la política. Gran Bretaña estaba imponiéndoles fuertes impuestos a las colonias. Uno de los productos gravados con impuestos era el té. Abigail pensaba que este impuesto era injusto y en su casa decidió servir café, en lugar de té.

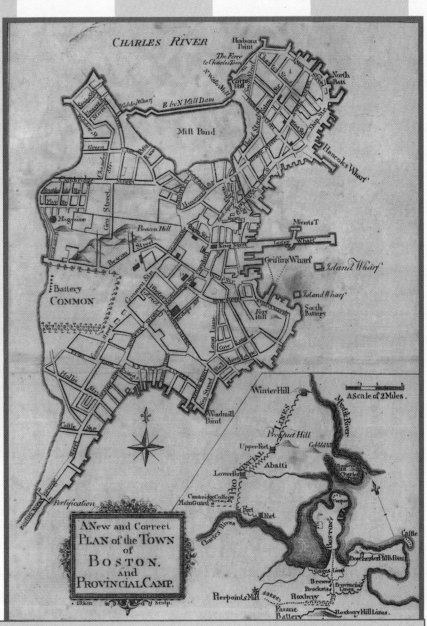

This map shows Boston, Massachusetts. Much of the early work of the American Revolution happened in Boston.

Mapa de Boston, Massachusetts. Gran parte del trabajo preparatorio de la Guerra de Independencia se hizo en Boston.

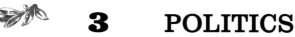

3 POLITICS

Many Americans felt the colonists should rule themselves. These people were called patriots. The people who wanted to stay part of Britain were loyalists. Abigail and John Adams were patriots. Abigail welcomed many important patriots to her home. She became friendly with Thomas Jefferson and Benjamin Franklin.

3 VIDA POLÍTICA

Muchos norteamericanos pensaban que las colonias debían gobernarse a sí mismas. A estas personas las llamaban "patriotas". A las personas que querían seguir siendo parte de Gran Bretaña las llamaban "realistas". Abigail y John Adams eran patriotas. Abigail recibió a muchos patriotas importantes en su casa y se hizo amiga de Thomas Jefferson y Benjamín Franklin.

Thomas Jefferson wrote the Declaration of Independence. He knew both John and Abigail Adams.

Thomas Jefferson escribió la Declaración de Independencia. Conocía a John y a Abigail Adams.

John Adams gave up his law practice for politics. He became a member of the Continental Congress. This group helped write the Declaration of Independence and the Constitution. The American Revolution started in 1775. John Adams traveled for much of that year.

John Adams dejó la carrera de abogado para dedicarse a la política. Se hizo miembro del Congreso Continental. Este grupo ayudó a escribir la Declaración de Independencia y la Constitución. La Guerra de Independencia comenzó en 1775. John Adams viajó durante gran parte de aquel año.

Benjamin Franklin helped write the Declaration of Independence and the Constitution.

Benjamín Franklin ayudó a escribir la Declaración de Independencia y la Constitución.

In 1778, John Adams was in France. After a brief visit home, he went to France again for five years. Abigail Adams ran the household while her husband was away. She did many tasks that women of that day did not usually do. She handled the farm's business and the household money. Abigail also made her home into a hospital for soldiers hurt in battles.

En 1778, John Adams trabajó en Francia. Luego de una breve visita a su hogar, regresó a Francia donde permaneció por cinco años. Abigail Adams se hizo cargo del hogar mientras su esposo estuvo fuera. Se encargaba de muchas tareas que las mujeres de la época por lo general no hacían. Estaba a cargo de la granja y del dinero del hogar. Abigail convirtió también su casa en hospital para los soldados heridos en las batallas.

Abigail wrote many letters to John Adams *(right)* while he was away in France *(map)*.

Abigail le escribió muchas cartas a John Adams *(derecha)* mientras él estuvo en Francia *(mapa)*.

4   FIRST LADY

In 1783, the American Revolution ended. Abigail Adams joined her husband in France. Traveling was hard in those days. The trip from Boston to England took four weeks by boat! Abigail's daughter, Nabby, traveled with her. The Adams family stayed in Europe until 1788. They tried to make things better between Britain and America.

---

4 PRIMERA DAMA

En 1783 terminó la Guerra de Independencia. Abigail Adams se unió a su esposo en Francia. En esos días viajar era difícil. ¡El viaje de Boston a Inglaterra duraba cuatro semanas en barco! La hija de Abigail, Nabby, viajó con ella. La familia Adams permaneció en Europa hasta 1788. Durante su estancia, trataron de mejorar las relaciones entre Gran Bretaña y Estados Unidos.

Abigail Amelia Adams Smith (1765–1813), known as Nabby, was the daughter of Abigail and John Adams.

Abigail Amelia Adams Smith (1765–1813), conocida como "Nabby", era hija de Abigail y John Adams.

In 1789, the Adams family sailed to New York. George Washington had chosen John Adams to be the vice president of the United States. Abigail Adams became good friends with Martha Washington. Martha was the first lady at that time.

En 1789, la familia Adams viajó a Nueva York. George Washington había elegido a John Adams para el cargo de vicepresidente de Estados Unidos. Abigail Adams se hizo buena amiga de Martha Washington. Martha era la primera dama en esa época.

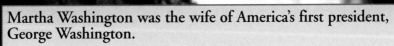

Martha Washington was the wife of America's first president, George Washington.

Martha Washington. Fue la esposa del primer presidente de Estados Unidos, George Washington.

5 VOICE FOR CHANGE

Abigail Adams was an independent woman. She was a working mother in an age when such women were uncommon. She raised her children and also ran the family's farm. There were many decisions to make in the running of a farm. Abigail had to hire workers and handle the sale of crops.

---

5 UNA VOZ A FAVOR DEL CAMBIO

Abigail Adams fue una mujer independiente. Era madre y además trabajaba, en una época en que esto era poco común. Criaba a sus hijos y también manejaba la granja de la familia. Cuando se maneja una granja hay que tomar muchas decisiones. Abigail contrataba a los trabajadores y se ocupaba de la venta de las cosechas.

LISPENARD'S MEADOWS.
Taken from the N.E.cor of the present Broadway & Spring St.
Drawn by A. Anderson, 1785.

These two etchings show farm life in the eighteenth century.

Ilustraciones que muestran la vida en las granjas en el siglo XVIII.

Abigail Adams did not see a big shift in women's rights in her lifetime. However, she was a voice for change. She spoke and wrote tirelessly about women's rights.

Abigail died on October 28, 1818, of a lung sickness. She was almost seventy-four years old. Many of Abigail's ideas came to pass years later.

Durante su vida, Abigail Adams no vio un gran cambio en lo que se refiere a los derechos de las mujeres. Sin embargo, fue una voz a favor del cambio. Habló y escribió sin descanso a favor de los derechos de las mujeres.

Abigail murió de una enfermedad pulmonar el 28 de octubre de 1818. Tenía casi setenta y cuatro años de edad. Años más tarde, muchas de sus ideas se hicieron realidad.

Abigail Adams died in her bed in 1818. She was the wife of one president and the mother of another.

Abigail Adams murió en su cama en 1818. Fue esposa de un presidente y madre de otro.

TIMELINE

1744—Abigail Smith is born.

1764—Abigail marries John Adams.

1784—Abigail and Nabby sail to England.

1785—The Adams family lives in France. John Quincy returns to America. John, Abigail, and Nabby move to England. John is named U.S. minister to Great Britain.

1789—John and Abigail sail to New York.

1797—John Adams becomes the second president of the United States.

1818—Abigail Adams dies.

CRONOLOGÍA

1744—Nace Abigail Smith.

1764—Abigail se casa con John Adams.

1784—Abigail y Nabby viajan a Inglaterra.

1785—La familia Adams vive en Francia. John Quincy regresa a Estados Unidos. John, Abigail y Nabby se mudan a Inglaterra cuando John es nombrado enviado de Estados Unidos ante Gran Bretaña.

1789—John y Abigail viajan a Nueva York.

1797—John Adams se convierte en el segundo presidente de Estados Unidos.

1818—Muere Abigail Adams.

30

GLOSSARY

American Revolution (uh-MER-uh-ken reh-vuh-LOO-shun)
Battles that soldiers from the colonies fought against Britain for freedom, from 1775 to 1783.

Constitution (kon-stih-TOO-shun) The basic rules by which the United States is governed.

Continental Congress (kon-tin-EN-tul KON-gres) A group, made up of a few men from every colony, that made decisions for the colonies.

independent (in-dih-PEN-dent) Free from the control or support of others.

WEB SITES

Due to the changing nature of Internet links, the Rosen Publishing Group, Inc., has developed an online list of Web sites related to the subject of this book. This site is updated regularly. Please use this link to access the list:

http://www.rosenlinks.com/fpah/aada

GLOSARIO

Congreso Continental (el) Grupo formado por unos cuantos hombres de cada colonia y que tomaba decisiones en representación de ellas.

Constitución (la) Las reglas básicas con las que se gobierna Estados Unidos.

Guerra de Independencia (la) La que libraron por la independencia los soldados de las colonias contra Gran Bretaña entre 1775 y 1783.

independiente Libre del control de otros.

SITIOS WEB

Debido a las constantes modificaciones en los sitios de Internet, Rosen Publishing Group, Inc., ha desarrollado un listado de sitios Web relacionados con el tema de este libro. Este sitio se actualiza con regularidad. Por favor, usa este enlace para acceder a la lista:

http://www.rosenlinks.com/fpah/aada

INDEX

ABOUT THE AUTHOR

Maya Glass is a writer and editor living in New York City.

ÍNDICE

ACERCA DEL AUTOR

Maya Glass es escritora y editora. Vive en la ciudad de Nueva York.